*The Organ Box*

Matt Howard

The Organ Box

First published in 2014 by Eyewear Publishing Ltd
74 Leith Mansions, Grantully Road
London W9 1LJ United Kingdom

Typeset with graphic design by Edwin Smet
Author photograph by Amanda Read
Printed in England by Lightning Source
All rights reserved © 2014 *Matt Howard*
The right of Matt Howard to be identified as author of this work has been asserted in accordance with section 77 of the Copyright, Designs and Patents Act 1988

ISBN 978-1-908998-61-3
WWW.EYEWEARPUBLISHING.COM

Thanks

I'd like to thank the following whose help and encouragement has been truly invaluable: Michael Mackmin, Michael Symmons Roberts, Jean Sprackland, Mark Cocker and all those in the 'The Butchery Group', Martin Figura and Helen Ivory, generous hosts and conveners and also my fellow members — Esther Morgan, Andrea Holland, Andrew McDonnell, Joanna Guthrie, Jonathan Morley and Tom Warner.

for Amanda

Table of contents

Making Evelyn's Tables

Omnia explorate; meliora retinete

It begins with a crime, a man dead,
outside of God. Then the felling of an evergreen,
a pine, from this they will make planks,
with tongue and groove to bind them, glued
with animal collagen from skin, tendon, hooves.
Last, a varnish: honey, cedar or poppy oil.

The man will be pinned in preparation,
his veins, nerves, arteries, set in a triptych.
He will display like a winter birch, each branch
bare of fruit, the crown wracked.
In the absence of viscera he will abstract
to the spaces between bone and flesh.

Then we will truly behold a man
for ourselves; trace the inner workings,
the circuit that oxygenates blood;
the sympathetic system of fight or flight,
endings that cause sweats, the heart to race,
stripped into lines of his feeling.

A jar of moles

I have trawled the whole city for your gift,
trusted the knowledge of black cabs to bring you this –
it is quite full, so be careful of its weight.

The man couldn't say how many it contains,
simply that it's full because it has to be,
just as a true heart only ever brims with love.

Each side is crammed with quiet wild faces,
pink snouts clear from their maze of dark chambers;
see, this one here still bares its teeth.

The labouring velvet behind blown glass through decades
and where one man made that emptiness
another has worked hard to fill it.

So take these moles darling, with my love,
hold them safe and away from the sun,
cherish each heavy earth-swimming hand.

To an anatomical Venus

Lady, you have no chest,
no stomach; the curtain of muscle
drawn, you are a reliquary, a trinket box,
faithful cavity of delicacies.

I pick out liver, kidney, spleen –
petals of your carnation, the heart
bright as a leaf from any book of hours.
Your maker has served you well.

I cannot meet your gaze or parted lips.
The comb of vessels on these neat lungs
suggests held breath, a promise –

a host of wax, braided with a wick
of real hair. I will not lift your womb;
the foetus, its honeyed silence.

The Devil's Letterbox

Now there is no fair weather, I'll work the hours west,
long miles of coffin path, then take the last turn south
past the end of the uplands hunched with granite churches,
to the peninsula, where belief is never more than elemental.

I'll find the pearl-eyed Bosun and barter
with flint ballast from the sea wall of our east coast
for use of his Missionary boat, then slip moorings
off Steeple Rock, far from this county's superstitions.

With all the piracy, the smuggled freight of my life,
I'll pilot the leer of that breaker's cove, spume and riptide,
to the bellows of the Devil's own letterbox.
Then unstow, against the rollers, for clemency,

post the folded bloodshirts of my father and brothers,
the charred words of my mother and sisters.
And in faith I come through, I'll look for news of you
in guano drifts and the brackish throats of gulls.

The anatomical storeroom inventory

I kick-off with a varnished shark's heart,
lion's toes and monkey faces,

you with the whole sea-horse,
its brood pouch peeled, full of eggs.

I reel off clubfoot, tapir's anus, a shotgun-blasted femur
and say how our intestines are just like sausage skin.

You suggest I'm heartless as that aortic arch
thickened with syphilitic aneurysm

and point me to *the concentric jewel* of a boar's epididymis,
the *complete votive* of a three-week old whale foetus.

I continue with a sequence of cock-sparrow testes,
though confuse the skin of bull's scrotum

with that of the finer Dura mater. You tick-off foot sole
of Homo sapiens, dissected, displaying the roots of a callus.

Gorilla gorilla gorilla

For Guy

For his moods,
the schemes and theories behind each curious held gaze,
the gasps and beating of his chest;
for his hands, their absolute power and grace;
every capture and release of sparrow or finch –
unharmed, their flight intensified.

For his obesity,
each of his thirty-four stones,
and his teeth, spoiled with melon, pineapple and dates,
even punnets of strawberries, sent out of season.
For his thirty one years
and the necessary dentistry that killed him.

For his dead weight in the deep freeze,
his pelt in the tanning drum,
the shrinkage of his skin and the beatitudes in his DNA;
the silver of his back that would not stretch for the stitching.
Guy on his haunches as full-mounted specimen.

For all the incinerated viscera,
the vanished waters of his eyes, their empty sockets;
for the painted glass beads
and the person who came by Circle Line to deliver them
and everyone they reflect; the irises too brown,
the too-perfect ring of each limbus.

A woman breastfeeding in the National Gallery

is crying and no one is ashamed to look as her face slips
its makeup. Almost boneless, just days after birth, here she is
concept, object d'art. Crying a fountain by the cloakroom,
she is less *Madonna of the Pinks*, more a Pietà.

That baby, its hunger; fists full of her puffed areola,
mouth of her pistil. Lily white and straggle-veined
she strains, an Empress squeezed into her old clothes.
Everyone looks; none can say enough is enough.

The House of Owls

The founding of the House of Owls

Before the many mothers, before the house,
her: she came with a heavy scent of hawthorn,
and all men were taken by her owl-white skin,

by such silent graces. She took just one
to the far meadow. He went meek as a harvest mouse.
Her garland of bluebell and yellow archangel slipped,

she bound his wrists with bindweed,
snicked stems of Jacob's ladder for their pillow.
On that unbroken earth she whispered:

Here we will have our many sons and daughters,
this is land to be taken, good ground for us to claim.
With each dead-nettle kiss she laid on his neck

a clutch of welts raised, never faded.
And in their godforsaken parish, this we know:
that ruin of a house still stands.

The true heir of the House of Owls

Born wrong, with an insatiable gape
and one odd tooth in a mask of a face.
It didn't so much cry as screech,

craved only for meat, begged
then swallowed whole. When it did settle,
it was into squeaks, snorts, hisses.

This firstborn came between them,
turned their bed into a midden,
a heap of fur, tails and tiny skulls.

He hadn't been near her in weeks.
When she caught him, three fields over,
whistling up at the lark, it was too far.

She waited with the child in its high chair
for when he came in that night, reeking of meadows –
met him with her black-marble stare:

Here my love, is how far a head can turn.
And with one hand on its shoulder,
one on the crown, she took that shrieking head,

twisted it past all turning.

A vision of order at the House of Owls

It was scryed again in the belly of a strung up pig.
They would have acres, far as the eye could see,
grazed and under plough; an estate for generations.

They worked hard for this gift.
Stone by insufferable stone, by the roots
of each felled tree; broke their backs every day.

He beasted a hound for coursing;
perfected the deadfall, birdlime and pole traps,
acquired breech-loading rifles.

He hanged one of each dead singer
from that immovable oak, where he carved her name
with those of all their children, born and yet to come.

The fall of the House of Owls, 1914

The man that came to cap the chimney stack
back then would have crossed a muddle of fields,
where his good word had beaten the bounds before him.
'Just a simple fix', he told her, 'a rough tile to point in'.
He marked year and initials by the trace of his fingertip.
By the smallest touches a house can fall.

A white feather chased two sons away,
then the front door lintel pocked with holes
where they say the mother, mad with hope,
nailed countless barn owl carcasses. Fields widened
and trunk roads drew close to the old routeways
where so many, blown sidewards, come to grief.

A century later contractors have come
and emptied the stack. A full three barrows.
A fallout of desiccated abundance; pellets crammed
with all that went with the meadows and hedgerows:
relics of frog, yellowhammer and dormouse;
Natterer's bat, water shrew and weasel.

The deliverer of the House of Owls

She has lived too long this way,
so old, deep into the monoculture of age.
On the brink like a slack-necked hatchling,

her bruised scalp flecked with white down
and the dangled quiver of those wasted arms –
one cold, wet wind could dash her away now.

On occasional days they bring her back,
though she can no longer make the stairs,
just sits in her chair by the picture window.

In between sleep her sunken face looks out,
twisted to the mute brown-green blur of fields.
And no word from her for nearly five years.

Yet that last night she woke the house with a shriek,
swore she saw a luminous owl with her bad eye,
lit with honey fungus, flying at the bounds of their acreage.

The Everyman Library in the University of Madrid

The English Brigaders were glad to have found it.
Editions in their own tongue, complete with jackets,
uncracked stiff spines; easy to stack for the Maxim nest
and other firing positions. Cheap but sturdy,
each one full of ideas, passion: *Great Expectations*,
On The Origin of Species, *The Prelude*; familiar names,
Donne, Tennyson, Keats. A docker from Toxteth
learned 'The Eagle' by heart. When fighting started
bullets struck the boards and rifled through,
and the works held their lines, inscribed
with new dedications, soaked from tunic pockets.

Today in the starving city of our liberation

No fish have been spared in the aquarium.
Rumours persist about the disappearance of cats.
That priest returned with his pocketful of denunciations,
requested a pistol and permit to carry it.

Three sisters with their heads shaved came from the hills,
reported something untranslatable regarding time with the priest
and were positively tremulous with some passion or injustice;
they left cider, or bad wine, and one blood-spotted egg.

The search of the catacombs continued
amidst accounts of knocking and scratching.
An obstinate monk was removed by force
and is now held in our cells on a charge of hoarding rats.

While the Mayor insisted with further papers of pure invention,
he left nothing but the smell of vegetables or dry rot
and claimed I wore the face of a hypocrite.
(I now fear all the more for the thinning flanks of his horse).

Just past lunch there was a bomb blast at the post office,
a time delayed fuse. One hundred dead. A tragedy –
so much plaster dust spoiled the raw flesh
of each halved tomato sun-drying in our courtyard.

Left glove

It's more like a gauntlet,
encrusted with soil and grass stains
that hold it, clawing the lawn,
caked in the workings of last year,
of all the years before.

Left with cast-out Christmas trees,
this glove has endured
the heavy onset of winter,
the garden's decay into brutish frosts
with fingers fused on the pulse

of each day's length, the scheduled
migrations. Warmed for a time
but abandoned. Poor, poor kapo
locked from the blockhouse shed,
sweated proxy for my soft hand's

exertions now grown around
by fallacious intimacies
of moss, web, leaf litter, weed.
The grass under the palm yellowed
like hay, made through the cold.

All this misses the point of order.
In my deeds there is clear delineation
of ownership and boundaries.
I bought this place from plans,
my hand in the design.

By this left glove I give
no forum, for this earth
has always been rough,
modern estates never quite lose
that construction site lay:

for each grass shoot or daffodil,
bloated bellies of flint,
unbroken or with a knapped edge;
shatterings of clay pipes,
plumb lines, nails and cable ties.

For this one glove left
another was thrown out
and a new pair bought in.
By my own soft hands
I stand here this spring,

where the grass grows
frayed at the seams I will work –
even through feast days, I will
dead-head roses, retrain, shear;
cut all back to fit my cloth.

Song Thrush

Les coquelicots B&B, Pozieres

He can barely fly. His khaki fatigues
soaked through, strung neck swathed
under beads; the one thrush seen all day.

Now, after incendiary sun, leaden rain,
there's only him singing to the premature dusk
over these fields and a handful of shuttered houses.

Here weather mobilises fast. Pressure
fronts collide over the open ground.
On the *circuit de souvenir* land is so fertile –

the earth must till itself.
Each season looses more swallowed
ordnance, still fused, for clearing.

After four-egg omelettes we play pool,
watch the teatime news in French.
He's out there, still on the wire in the dark,

head gone, cold rain rising in hollow bones
singing; not for romance or what's behind
or ahead; a pure lyric for his moment only,

just a chance a chance a chance.

Regression to the mean

Equally applicable to men, brutes and plants.

Sir Francis Galton

Washing your hair, I'm always struck
how my right hand is like a calliper,
little finger and thumb, weighing your forehead.
Sick again, I have scrubbed you long enough

to exfoliate bone. Such congested eugenics
at bath time; your head lolls like a late daffodil –
your sparrow lungs are brisk with a crow's hack.
Impatient as ever, my back and calves ache.

Our ritual bickering glossolalia.
My puffed fingertips are peelable now,
a fault of the skin in water; each whorl

unfathomable as the efficacy of prayer
or how this water moves, its gravity waves
reassembling my face like a photofit.

Acquired deformities: Constriction of female thorax

Presented by Sir Erasmus Wilson, 1884

Preserved the way you were wanted,
wasp-waisted, deformed from years of corsetry,
cartilage and ribs drawn oblique
like tight lace. The curve in the spine,
once pliable, fused here,
a lifelong pinch to angle the bust.

Diminutive even in your glass case
all I have are metaphors for you:
your wicker ribs an empty fruit basket
or a beekeeper's straw skep, colonised
then smoked out by men's words for sweetness –
caught in the vice of their love; concertina of bones.

That I could hold you now, ease this organ box,
free each reed, feel you breathe.

The drawer of kingfishers

In a row of study skins, the closest thing
to the bird is this single left wing:
Shot on the jetty at Rollesby.
You can run your finger and thumb
along the curve of feather and bone –

vane and current. A water-bracer;
hilt of a king's stiletto
in a slow lowland river
that breaks with the catch; a struck match
at the corner in the blue of your eye.

Datum

You left a glass of near-turned milk
by the front door to draw a ghost.
We had talked late and of everything.

Sleep was a cold confusion of birds,
the stuck chink of a chaffinch,
robins ticking incessant at the edge

of territory. Ice set hard as pig iron.
We walked there, found him in time
enough to barely hear movement:

grace notes of snow falling after
the fall; slips from the hedgerow –
the faint yield and hold of flakes

crumpling in the ditch bottom
where he struggled, naked as a miracle.
There was no explanation, just warm hands

on near translucent skin, his spider-work
of veins – blue crystallite blooms,
the spindly ribs borne kneading between us.

This other must have fallen clear through,
himself under some misalignment, the frost
hoar masking true punctuation of the fixed stars.

We held him in that dream, our loosed heat
thawing the geometry of his face,
his first-last words: *now I know of gravity.*

Acknowledgements

Acknowledgements are due to the editors of the following publications in which some of these poems have appeared: *The Rialto, The Dark Horse, Poetry Salzburg Review, Magma* and *Stand.*

'To an anatomical Venus' was highly commended in the 2012 International Hippocrates Prize for Poetry and Medicine Open Category.

EYEWEAR PAMPHLET SERIES

BEN STAINTON EDIBLES
MEL PRYOR DRAWN ON WATER
MICHAEL BROWN UNDERSONG
MATT HOWARD THE ORGAN BOX
RACHAEL M NICHOLAS SOMEWHERE NEAR IN THE DARK
BETH TICHBORNE HUNGRY FOR AIR
GALE BURNS OPAL EYE

EYEWEAR POETRY

MORGAN HARLOW MIDWEST RITUAL BURNING
KATE NOAKES CAPE TOWN
RICHARD LAMBERT NIGHT JOURNEY
SIMON JARVIS EIGHTEEN POEMS
ELSPETH SMITH DANGEROUS CAKES
CALEB KLACES BOTTLED AIR
GEORGE ELLIOTT CLARKE ILLICIT SONNETS
HANS VAN DE WAARSENBURG THE PAST IS NEVER DEAD
DAVID SHOOK OUR OBSIDIAN TONGUES
BARBARA MARSH TO THE BONEYARD
MARIELA GRIFFOR THE PSYCHIATRIST
DON SHARE UNION
SHEILA HILLIER HOTEL MOONMILK
FLOYD SKLOOT CLOSE READING
PENNY BOXALL SHIP OF THE LINE
MANDY KAHN MATH, HEAVEN, TIME
MARION MCCREADY TREE LANGUAGE
RUFO QUINTAVALLE WEATHER DERIVATIVES
SJ FOWLER THE ROTTWEILER'S GUIDE TO THE DOG OWNER
TEDI LÓPEZ MILLS DEATH ON RUA AUGUSTA
AGNIESZKA STUDZINSKA WHAT THINGS ARE
JEMMA BORG THE ILLUMINATED WORLD
KEIRAN GODDARD FOR THE CHORUS
COLETTE SENSIER SKINLESS

EYEWEAR PROSE

SUMIA SUKKAR THE BOY FROM ALEPPO WHO PAINTED THE WAR
ALFRED CORN MIRANDA'S BOOK

EYEWEAR LITERARY CRITICISM

MARK FORD DIALOGUE OF ONE

Lightning Source UK Ltd.
Milton Keynes UK
UKOW06f0722210815

257267UK00002B/7/P

9 781908 998613